For Elizabeth—we celebrate you.
—JY & HEYS

To Erin and Xiaoqing, you are the light of my life.
—JC

Special thanks to our expert readers who provided feedback on
the text and illustrations in the context of their own experiences:
Manan Bhandari, Dr. Lindsay Dubbs, Rabbi Jeni Friedman, Ivana Lee,
Sanyukta Mathur, Amber Williams, and Rev. Jin Haeng Kai Wiswall.

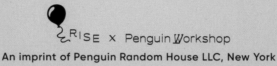

RISE x Penguin Workshop

An imprint of Penguin Random House LLC, New York

First published in the United States of America by Rise × Penguin Workshop,
an imprint of Penguin Random House LLC, New York, 2024

Visit us online at penguinrandomhouse.com.

Library of Congress Cataloging-in-Publication Data is available.

Manufactured in China

ISBN 9780593752296   10 9 8 7 6 5 4 3 2 1 HH

The text is set in Gilroy and Accolade.
The art was created digitally in Photoshop with a tablet.

Edited by Cecily Kaiser
Art Directed by Meagan Bennett and Maria Elias
Designed by Meagan Bennett

We Celebrate the Light

by Jane Yolen and Heidi E. Y. Stemple

illustrated by Jieting Chen

RISE

NEW YORK

DIWALI

When the days get shorter
and the night sneaks in early,

we celebrate the light.

DIWALI is the five-day Hindu celebration of light and the new year.

When we gather together,
we celebrate family.

When we tell our stories and sing our songs,
we celebrate the earth's turning.

The **WINTER SOLSTICE** is the shortest day of the year, when the sun rises late and sets early, which is celebrated by many cultures around the world.

When we decorate our doors, windows, chimneys, and houses, we celebrate our homes.
Where we live today and others that hold memories.

When we look at the pictures
of those who came before us,
we celebrate love.

And loss.

CHRISTMAS is the Christian celebration of the birth of Christ.

When we play our games, we celebrate joy and friendship and togetherness.

CHANUKAH is the Jewish celebration of a great miracle that happened a long time ago: Just a small bit of oil that was used to light lamps lasted eight whole nights.

When we set our tables,
filling our plates with feasts
that our ancestors ate,

we celebrate the
sweet and the bitter,
unity and separation.

Bountiful harvests
from the rich soil.

KWANZAA is the weeklong celebration of African and African American culture and the unity of all Black people, living all over the world.

When we honor traditions,
we celebrate our people's long history.

The good, the bad, the losses, the gains . . .

. . . and the hopeful
days to come.

BODHI DAY marks the moment the Buddha found enlightenment after forty-nine days of meditation, and is celebrated by Buddhists as they slow down to enjoy inner peace and the natural world around them.

BODHI DAY

When we say our prayers,
we speak to the Almighty,
the Ultimate, our Mother Earth.

And to our own
loving hearts.

When we go to bed
after the feast,
after the day of prayers
and remembrance,
after the celebration—

we wake to a lighter day,
a bigger heart,
and a world that holds
us together once again.

We celebrate the light.

LUNAR NEW YEAR is an Asian celebration lasting for more than two weeks that begins at the start of a new year of moon cycles and ends with a Lantern Festival as the earth moves back toward the sun.

Many families celebrate holidays during the late fall and winter. While our traditions may vary, the light and love that we honor unites us all.

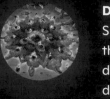

DIWALI is the Indian Hindu, Jain, and Sikh holiday honoring the god Rama and the triumph of good over evil, or light over darkness. It's celebrated over five days, during which houses are cleaned, special foods (both sweet and savory) are enjoyed, and fireworks light the sky. Many families create *rangoli* (art made from natural materials) and light *diyas* (clay lamps).

SOLSTICE is the celebration of the turning of the seasons. The winter solstice is celebrated on the shortest day of the year with the least amount of sun and light. Many families and communities gather outside to honor their connection to nature and the earth.

CHRISTMAS is the Christian celebration of the birth of Jesus Christ. There are many Christian religions and lots of different ways to celebrate. Many families celebrate together by going to church, singing carols, and decorating their homes with strings of lights. Some hang stockings for Santa Claus to fill with gifts while they sleep, and brightly wrapped presents are placed under a twinkling pine tree.

CHANUKAH is the eight-day Jewish holiday celebrating the miracle of lamp oil lasting much longer than expected. Candles in the menorah are lit each night, using the *shammash* (center) candle to light the others while reciting prayers. Many families eat food cooked in oil, such as fried potato pancakes (*latkes*) and doughnuts (*sufganiyot*), and play *dreidel*, a spinning top with Hebrew characters.

KWANZAA is a weeklong holiday celebrating the culture, history, community, and family of African and Pan-African people (those of African descent living all over the world). Many families gather, make crafts, tell stories, reflect, and feast. Seven candles in black, red, and green are lit, representing the seven core principles of Kwanzaa. At the table, a unity cup, symbolic of the first principle (*umoja*), is raised and shared.

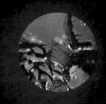

BODHI DAY is a Buddhist holiday celebrating the day the Buddha reached enlightenment—a deep understanding of the world—after forty-nine days of meditation. Many families celebrate by decorating a bodhi or Ficus tree with colorful lights and meditating. The traditional meal is a rice and milk dish that is similar to what the Buddha ate after his long fast.

LUNAR NEW YEAR (sometimes called Chinese New Year or Spring Festival) is celebrated by almost every Asian culture around the world. Fifteen days of celebration begin on the first new moon of the lunar year. Many families gather together and welcome the New Year with a feast. Some celebrations include red envelopes filled with cash given as gifts to children, and everyone stays up late to welcome the New Year. The celebration ends on the first full moon of the year with the Lantern Festival, where dancers dressed as dragons perform a dance surrounded by colorful lanterns for good fortune.